Marshmallows

MADE MARVELLOUS

LOVE FOOD™

Contents

Pina Colada Marshmallows 46

Mojito Marshmallows 48

Bourbon & Brown Sugar Marshmallows 50

Amaretto Crunch Marshmallows 52

Irish Cream Marshmallows 54

Egg Nog Marshmallows 56

Rum & Raisin Marshmallows 58

Toffee Apple Marshmallow Pops 60

Pumpkin & Pecan Marshmallows 64

Peanut Butter & Jelly Marshmallows 66

Gingerbread Marshmallows 68

Cookies & Cream Marshmallows 70

S'mores Marshmallow Pops 72

Zesty Lemon Marshmallows 76

Mad about
MARSHMALLOWS

Introduction

MARSHMALLOWS ARE THE HOTTEST NEW TREND IN THE WORLD OF HOME-MADE CONFECTIONERY — AND IF YOU THOUGHT THESE LIGHT-AS-AIR PILLOWS OF SUGARY SWEETNESS WERE TOO TRICKY TO MAKE YOURSELF, THEN THINK AGAIN!

All of the marshmallows in this book are based on one basic recipe. Hone your mallow-making skills and familiarize yourself with the terminology and techniques using the basic recipe (page 12), then expand your repertoire to include the more indulgent variations that follow. With a huge selection of shapes, flavours and finishing flourishes (which you can pick and mix to create your own maverick marshmallows) you really are spoilt for choice.

Top tips for sweet success

MARSHMALLOW MAKING IS ALL DOWN TO TIMING SO IT'S ESSENTIAL TO HAVE EVERYTHING READY BEFORE YOU START. FIRST PREPARE THE TIN OR MOULDS, THEN ACCURATELY WEIGH ALL THE INGREDIENTS. DISSOLVE THE GELATINE WHILE THE SUGAR SYRUP IS BOILING, THEN, JUST BEFORE THE SYRUP REACHES THE FIRM-BALL STAGE, START WHISKING THE EGG WHITES.

○ **To achieve a crystal-clear syrup, make sure that the sugar is completely dissolved in the liquid before slowly bringing it to the boil. Don't stir the boiling syrup as this will make it become cloudy and grainy.**

○ **When dissolving the gelatine, use hot (not boiling) liquid and stir for 1-2 minutes until the grains have dissolved. If any small lumps of gelatine remain, place the bowl into a larger bowl of hot water and stir until the liquid is clear.**

○ **Add the hot syrup and gelatine to the whisked egg whites in a slow and steady stream. Try to make sure the syrup hits the egg whites and not the whisk blades or the sides of the bowl where it will set instantly.**

○ **When all the syrup has been whisked into the egg whites increase the speed of the mixer and whisk continuously for about 10 minutes – the mixture will increase in volume and become thick and glossy.**

○ **Setting times will vary depending on the size of tin or mould used, as well as the flavouring added. Dust the uppermost surface with a little more of the coating mixture – this will stop it from drying out too much whilst setting. Leave the marshmallow to set in a cool dry place, but do not put it in the refrigerator.**

○ **If you don't want to cut the set marshmallow straight away, lift it out of the tin using the lining paper and place it in a large, airtight container. Do not remove the lining paper until you are ready to cut and coat the marshmallow.**

Keeping qualities

ALTHOUGH BEST EATEN WITHIN A COUPLE OF DAYS OF MAKING, UNDECORATED MARSHMALLOWS (WITHOUT A COATING LIKE CHOCOLATE OR CARAMEL) WILL EASILY KEEP FOR UP TO 5 DAYS. STORE IN AN AIRTIGHT CONTAINER IN A COOL, DRY PLACE. MARSHMALLOWS ALSO FREEZE EXCEPTIONALLY WELL. FREEZE IN A SINGLE LAYER IN A FREEZER-PROOF CONTAINER FOR UP TO 1 MONTH. DEFROST AT ROOM TEMPERATURE FOR 30 MINUTES–1 HOUR, DEPENDING ON THE SIZE.

Essential ingredients

Sugar

Everyday granulated sugar is ideal for the basic sugar syrup. The even-sized grains will slowly dissolve into the liquid when gently heated.

Egg whites

Always use fresh eggs at room temperature. Chilled egg whites will not incorporate as much air when whisked, so remember to remove the eggs from the refrigerator at least 30 minutes before you start cooking.

Gelatine

Powdered gelatine (as used in all of the recipes that follow) dissolved in hot water gives the marshmallow its soft set and springy texture. Always add the gelatine into the liquid, never the other way round, or it won't dissolve properly.

Icing sugar and cornflour

All marshmallows need to be lightly coated with a mix of icing sugar and cornflour to prevent them from sticking to absolutely everything! Use equal quantities of each and sift together through a fine sieve to remove any small lumps.

Veggie friendly

There are vegetarian alternatives to powdered gelatine available – follow packet instructions to prepare, then add to the sugar syrup in place of the gelatine solution.

Basic equipment

Food mixer

The secret to a light and voluminous marshmallow mixture is to whisk, whisk, whisk! If you plan to make a lot of marshmallows, then a freestanding mixer with a whisk attachment is essential. A hand-held mixer will do the job just as well, as long as it has variable speed settings.

Sugar thermometer

To make sure that the sugar syrup is boiled to the correct temperature you'll need to invest in a sugar thermometer. The syrup needs to reach the 'firm ball' stage which will be clearly marked on the thermometer.

Heavy-based saucepan

Use a medium-sized heavy-based saucepan to make the sugar syrup. It needs to be deep enough for the sugar thermometer to clip to the side of the pan without touching the base.

Heatproof bowls and jug

These are essential as the boiled sugar syrup is extremely hot and will melt plastic equipment. To pour the hot syrup into the whisked egg whites in a steady stream use a large heatproof jug with a firm handle.

Cake tins and silicone moulds

The marshmallow mixture needs to be set in a shallow tin or mould. Always prepare by greasing thoroughly with a flavourless oil or non-stick cooking spray. Line with baking paper, then re-grease and dust with the cornflour and icing sugar mixture. Silicone cake tins or individual silicone cases have the added benefit of being very flexible, so the set marshmallows are really easy to remove.

Sharp knife

A long, thin-bladed sharp knife will make light work of cutting the set marshmallow into pieces. It needs to be lightly greased to prevent sticking. Alternatively, a greased pizza cutter or a pair of sharp scissors will also do the job.

Cookie cutters

Marshmallow that has been set in a Swiss roll tin is thin enough to be stamped out in shapes using cookie cutters. Choose simple shapes and use a pastry brush to thoroughly grease the cutter. Press the cutter down firmly with the palm of your hand, then gently lift out the shaped marshmallow.

Safety first

Of course, common sense rules in the kitchen (especially when you're working with hot sugar). Take care when boiling the syrup and adding it to the egg whites as it will be extremely hot!

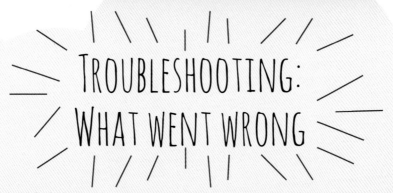

TROUBLESHOOTING:
WHAT WENT WRONG

MARSHMALLOW MUDDLE: **Help! There are sugar crystals in the syrup.**
SUPER-SWEET SOLUTION: **The sugar was not thoroughly dissolved in the liquid or the syrup was stirred during boiling. To prevent sugar crystals forming on the inside of the saucepan brush lightly with cold water just above the bubbling syrup.**

MARSHMALLOW MUDDLE: **Oh no! My marshmallow mixture isn't increasing in volume!**
SUPER-SWEET SOLUTION: **All the air was knocked out of the egg whites when the hot syrup was added too quickly. Add the syrup in a very slow trickle at the start, then in a thicker stream as the volume of the mixture increases.**

MARSHMALLOW MUDDLE: **Why are my marshmallows so dense?**
SUPER-SWEET SOLUTION: **The mixture was not whisked for long enough or was over-beaten after the flavourings were added.**

MARSHMALLOW MUDDLE: **My 'mallows went soggy in storage...**
SUPER-SWEET SOLUTION: **The mixture was not whisked for long enough. If this doesn't work, try reducing the volume of liquid used for softening the gelatine, but only by 1–2 tablespoons.**

FEATHER-LIGHT,
fluffy, puffy treats

Basic Vanilla
MARSHMALLOWS

Ingredients

SUNFLOWER OIL, FOR GREASING

1 TBSP CORNFLOUR

1 TBSP ICING SUGAR

200 ML/7 FL OZ COLD WATER

450 G/1 LB GRANULATED SUGAR

100 ML/3½ FL OZ HOT WATER

25 G/1 OZ POWDERED GELATINE

2 LARGE EGG WHITES

1 TSP VANILLA EXTRACT

1. Lightly oil a 20-cm/8-inch shallow square cake tin. Line the base and two sides with baking paper, then lightly oil the paper.

2. To make the coating, sift together the cornflour and icing sugar into a bowl. Use a little of this mixture to dust the lined tin, tapping it firmly so the mixture coats the base and sides completely.

3. To make the marshmallow, put the cold water and granulated sugar into a small deep saucepan. Heat gently, stirring constantly with a wooden spoon, until the sugar has dissolved.

4. Bring the syrup to the boil and boil, without stirring, for about 5 minutes until the mixture reaches around 120°C/248°F on a sugar thermometer (the firm ball stage).

5. Meanwhile, put the hot water into a small bowl, sprinkle over the gelatine and stir until dissolved and the liquid is clear. Put the egg whites into the bowl of a free-standing electric mixer and whisk until they hold stiff peaks.

6. When the syrup has reached the correct temperature, remove the pan from the heat and add the gelatine mixture – it will fizz and bubble. Leave to stand for a few seconds, then slowly pour the syrup into a large, heatproof jug (take care because the mixture will be extremely hot).

...CONTINUES ON PAGE 14

12

2.

4.

5.

6.

7.

7. Switch on the mixer on low speed and gradually add the hot syrup to the egg whites in a slow thin stream, whisking constantly. When all the syrup has been added increase the speed to high and whisk for 10 minutes until the mixture is very thick and glossy and leaves a thick trail on the surface when the whisk is lifted.

8. Whisk in the vanilla extract.

9. Pour the mixture into the prepared tin and use a spatula to gently level the surface.

10. Lightly dust the top with a little of the coating mixture. Leave to set, uncovered, in a cool, dry place for 4–5 hours.

11. Run the tip of a lightly greased knife along the unlined sides of the tin to release the marshmallow. Using the lining paper, gently lift out the marshmallow and place on a chopping board.

12. Cut into 25 or 36 squares, frequently wiping and re-greasing the knife. Lightly dust the squares with the remaining coating mixture. Store in an airtight container for up to 5 days.

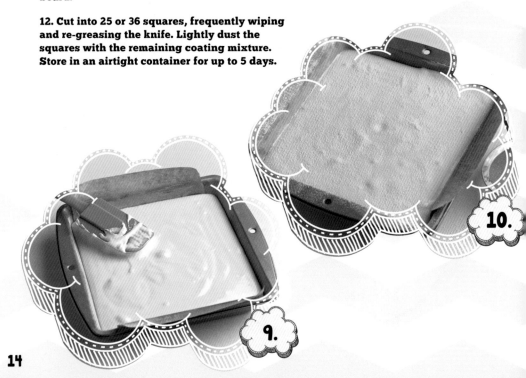

9.

10.

Very Vanilla
MARSHMALLOW TOPPERS

Ingredients

SUNFLOWER OIL, FOR GREASING

1 TBSP CORNFLOUR

1 TBSP ICING SUGAR

200 ML/7 FL OZ COLD WATER

450 G/1 LB GRANULATED SUGAR

100 ML/3½ FL OZ HOT WATER

25 G/1 OZ POWDERED GELATINE

2 LARGE EGG WHITES

1 TSP VANILLA EXTRACT

COCOA POWDER, FOR DUSTING

1. Lightly oil a 23 x 33-cm/9 x 13-inch Swiss roll tin. Line the base and two short sides with baking paper, then lightly oil the paper.

2. To make the coating, sift together the cornflour and icing sugar into a bowl. Use a little of this mixture to dust the lined tin, tapping it firmly so the mixture coats the base and sides completely.

3. Follow the basic recipe (see page 12) to make the marshmallow. Pour the mixture into the prepared tin and gently level the surface. Lightly dust the top with a little of the coating mixture. Leave to set, uncovered, in a cool, dry place for 3-4 hours.

4. Run the tip of a lightly greased knife along the unlined sides of the tin to release the marshmallow. Using the lining paper, gently lift out the marshmallow sheet and place on a chopping board.

5. Lightly grease a large snowflake cookie cutter and use to stamp out 14 shapes, washing, drying and re-greasing the cutter frequently. Use a small star-shaped cutter to stamp out about 10 stars from the remaining marshmallow. Toss all the shapes in the remaining coating mixture. Store in an airtight container for up to 5 days.

6. To serve, dust with cocoa powder and float the marshmallows on top of hot drinks such as milky coffee or hot chocolate.

3.

5.

6.

Milk Chocolate
MARSHMALLOW STIRRERS

Makes: 25
Prep: 45 minutes
(plus cooling)
Cook: 25 minutes
Set: 4-5 hours

Ingredients

SUNFLOWER OIL, FOR GREASING

1 TBSP CORNFLOUR

1 TBSP ICING SUGAR

200 ML/7 FL OZ COLD WATER

450 G/1 LB GRANULATED SUGAR

100 ML/3½ FL OZ HOT WATER

25 G/1 OZ POWDERED GELATINE

2 LARGE EGG WHITES

1 TSP VANILLA EXTRACT

TO DECORATE

150 G/5½ OZ MILK CHOCOLATE,
BROKEN INTO PIECES

HUNDREDS AND THOUSANDS

YOU WILL ALSO NEED

25 LOLLIPOP STICKS

1. Lightly oil an 18-cm/7-inch square cake tin (at least 5 cm/2 inches deep). Line the base and two sides with baking paper, then lightly oil the paper.

2. To make the coating, sift together the cornflour and icing sugar into a bowl. Use a little of this mixture to dust the lined tin, tapping it firmly so the mixture coats the base and sides completely.

3. Follow the basic recipe (see page 12) to make the marshmallow. Pour the mixture into the prepared tin and gently level the surface. Lightly dust with a little of the coating mixture. Leave to set, uncovered, in a cool, dry place for 4-5 hours.

4. Run the tip of a lightly greased knife along the unlined sides of the tin to release the marshmallow. Using the lining paper, gently lift out the marshmallow and place on a chopping board. Cut into 25 squares with a lightly greased knife. Lightly dust the squares with the remaining coating mixture.

5. To decorate, put the chocolate into a heatproof bowl set over a saucepan of gently simmering water and heat until melted. Remove from the heat and stir until smooth. Leave to cool for 10 minutes.

6. Gently push a lollipop stick into each marshmallow. Dip in the melted chocolate, turning to coat, then shake gently to allow the excess to run off.

7. Roll each dipped marshmallow in the hundreds and thousands to coat. Place on a baking sheet lined with baking paper and leave in a cool place to set. Store in an airtight container for up to 5 days.

Pink & Puffy
MARSHMALLOW CRISPS

Makes: 24
Prep: 45 minutes
(plus cooling)
Cook: 20 minutes
Set: 3-4 hours

Ingredients

SUNFLOWER OIL, FOR GREASING

1 TBSP CORNFLOUR

1 TBSP ICING SUGAR

200 ML/7 FL OZ COLD WATER

450 G/1 LB GRANULATED SUGAR

100 ML/3½ FL OZ HOT WATER

25 G/1 OZ POWDERED GELATINE

2 LARGE EGG WHITES

1 TSP VANILLA EXTRACT

PINK FOOD COLOURING PASTE

75 G/2¾ OZ PUFFED RICE CEREAL

1. Lightly oil a 23 x 33-cm/9 x 13-inch Swiss roll tin. Line the base and two short sides with baking paper, then lightly oil the paper. Line a large baking sheet with baking paper.

2. To make the coating, sift together the cornflour and icing sugar into a bowl. Use a little of this mixture to dust the lined tin, tapping it firmly so the mixture coats the base and sides completely.

3. Follow the basic recipe (see page 12) to make the marshmallow. Add a little of the food colouring paste to colour the mixture pale pink, then fold in the cereal. Pour the mixture into the prepared tin and gently level the surface. Lightly dust the top with a little of the coating mixture. Leave to set, uncovered, in a cool, dry place for 3–4 hours.

4. Run the tip of a lightly greased knife along the unlined sides of the tin to release the marshmallow. Using the lining paper, gently lift out the marshmallow sheet and place on a chopping board.

5. Lightly grease a 5-cm/2-inch round cutter and use to stamp out 24 rounds, washing, drying and re-greasing the cutter frequently. Toss the rounds in the remaining coating mixture. Store in an airtight container for up to 2 days.

YOU CAN MAKE MARSHMALLOW CRISPS WITH ANY OF THE FLAVOURED MARSHMALLOW RECIPES THAT FOLLOW – JUST ADD PUFFED RICE CEREAL TO THE MIXTURE!

Rainbow Stripe
MARSHMALLOWS

Makes: 36
Prep: 50 minutes
Cook: 20 minutes
Set: 4–5 hours

Ingredients

SUNFLOWER OIL, FOR GREASING

1 TBSP CORNFLOUR

1 TBSP ICING SUGAR

200 ML/7 FL OZ COLD WATER

450 G/1 LB GRANULATED SUGAR

100 ML/3½ FL OZ HOT WATER

25 G/1 OZ POWDERED GELATINE

2 LARGE EGG WHITES

1 TSP VANILLA EXTRACT

VIOLET, PINK, GREEN AND ORANGE
FOOD COLOURING PASTE

1. Lightly oil a 20-cm/8-inch shallow square cake tin. Line the base and two sides with baking paper, then lightly oil the paper.

2. To make the coating, sift together the cornflour and icing sugar into a bowl. Use a little of this mixture to dust the lined tin, tapping it firmly so the mixture coats the base and sides completely.

3. Follow the basic recipe (see page 12) to make the marshmallow. Divide the mixture evenly between four small bowls. Whisk a little violet food colouring paste into one bowl. Spoon the coloured marshmallow into the base of the prepared tin and gently level the surface with a small angled palette knife.

4. Repeat the colouring and layering with the remaining bowls of mixture to create a rainbow effect. Work quickly before the marshmallow starts to set. Lightly dust the top layer of the marshmallow with a little of the coating mixture. Leave to set, uncovered, in a cool, dry place for 4–5 hours.

5. Run the tip of a lightly greased knife along the unlined sides of the tin to release the marshmallow. Using the lining paper, gently lift out the marshmallow and place on a chopping board.

6. Cut into 36 squares, wiping and re-greasing the knife frequently. Lightly dust the squares with the remaining coating mixture. Store in an airtight container for up to 5 days.

3.

4.

6.

Sweetheart
MARSHMALLOW POPS

Makes: 25
Prep: 55 minutes (plus cooling)
Cook: 25 minutes
Set: 3–4 hours

Ingredients

SUNFLOWER OIL, FOR GREASING

1 TBSP CORNFLOUR

1 TBSP ICING SUGAR

200 ML/7 FL OZ COLD WATER

450 G/1 LB GRANULATED SUGAR

100 ML/3½ FL OZ HOT WATER

25 G/1 OZ POWDERED GELATINE

2 LARGE EGG WHITES

2 TSP ROSEWATER

PINK FOOD COLOURING PASTE

TO DECORATE

400 G/14 OZ PINK CANDY MELTS

HUNDREDS AND THOUSANDS

YOU WILL ALSO NEED

25 LOLLIPOP STICKS

PINK OR RED RIBBON

1. Lightly oil a 23 x 33-cm/9 x 13-inch Swiss roll tin. Line the base and two short sides with baking paper, then lightly oil the paper.

2. To make the coating, sift together the cornflour and icing sugar into a bowl. Use a little of this mixture to dust the lined tin, tapping it firmly so the mixture coats the base and sides completely.

3. Follow the basic recipe (see page 12) to make the marshmallow, replacing the vanilla extract with rosewater. Colour the mixture pale pink with a little food colouring paste. Pour the mixture into the prepared tin and gently level the surface. Lightly dust the top with a little of the coating mixture. Leave to set, uncovered, in a cool, dry place for 3–4 hours.

4. Run the tip of a lightly greased knife along the unlined sides of the tin to release the marshmallow. Using the lining paper, gently lift out the marshmallow sheet and place on a chopping board.

5. Lightly grease a 4.5-cm/1³/₄-inch heart-shaped cutter and use to stamp out 25 hearts, washing, drying and re-greasing the cutter frequently. Toss the hearts in the remaining coating mixture.

...CONTINUES ON PAGE 26

3.

3.

6.

6. To decorate, place the candy melts in a large heatproof bowl set over a saucepan of gently simmering water and leave until melted. Remove from the heat and stir until smooth. Leave to cool for 5 minutes.

7. Using two spoons, quickly dip each marshmallow heart in the melted mixture, turning to coat completely. Place on a large baking sheet lined with baking paper and sprinkle with hundreds and thousands. Leave in a cool, dry place to set.

8. Carefully remove the hearts from the baking paper and gently push a lollipop stick into the base of each heart. Tie a ribbon bow onto each stick. Store in an airtight container for up to 5 days.

IF A VALENTINE'S VIBE DOESN'T TICKLE YOUR FANCY, GIVE THESE DELICATE ROSEWATER POPS SOME PETAL-POWER WITH A FLOWER-SHAPED COOKIE CUTTER.

OH SO CUTE!

27

Chai Tea & Vanilla
MINI MARSHMALLOWS

Makes: 50
Prep: 40 minutes
Cook: 20 minutes
Set: 3-4 hours

Ingredients

SUNFLOWER OIL, FOR GREASING

1 TBSP CORNFLOUR

1 TBSP ICING SUGAR

1/2 TSP GROUND GINGER

1/2 TSP GROUND CLOVES

100 ML/31/2 FL OZ COLD WATER

100 ML/31/2 FL OZ COLD CHAI TEA, MADE WITH 1 CHAI TEABAG

450 G/1 LB GRANULATED SUGAR

100 ML/31/2 FL OZ HOT WATER

25 G/1 OZ POWDERED GELATINE

2 LARGE EGG WHITES

1 TSP VANILLA EXTRACT

1 TSP GROUND CARDAMOM AND 1 TSP GRATED NUTMEG, FOR SPRINKLING

1. Lightly oil a 23 x 33-cm/9 x 13-inch Swiss roll tin. Line the base and two short sides with baking paper, then lightly oil the paper.

2. To make the coating, sift together the cornflour, icing sugar, ginger and cloves into a bowl. Use a little of this mixture to dust the lined tin, tapping it firmly so the mixture coats the base and sides completely.

3. Follow the basic recipe (see page 12) to make the marshmallow, replacing half the cold water for the sugar syrup with the chai tea.

4. Pour the mixture into the prepared tin and gently level the surface. Sprinkle over the cardamom and nutmeg then lightly dust the top with a little of the coating mixture. Leave to set, uncovered, in a cool, dry place for 3-4 hours.

5. Run the tip of a lightly greased knife along the unlined sides of the tin to release the marshmallow. Using the lining paper, gently lift out the marshmallow sheet and place on a chopping board.

6. Using a lightly greased mini star-shaped cutter, stamp out about 50 shapes, washing, drying and re-greasing the cutter frequently. Toss the shapes in the remaining coating mixture. Store in an airtight container for up to 5 days.

Peanut Butter Cup
MARSHMALLOWS

Makes: 42
Prep: 45 minutes
(plus cooling)
Cook: 25 minutes
Set: 2-3 hours

Ingredients

SUNFLOWER OIL, FOR GREASING

1 TBSP CORNFLOUR

1 TBSP ICING SUGAR

200 ML/7 FL OZ COLD WATER

450 G/1 LB GRANULATED SUGAR

100 ML/3½ FL OZ HOT WATER

25 G/1 OZ POWDERED GELATINE

2 LARGE EGG WHITES

1 TSP VANILLA EXTRACT

85 G/3 OZ CHOPPED MIXED NUTS

TO DECORATE

200 G/7 OZ MILK CHOCOLATE,
BROKEN INTO PIECES

55 G/2 OZ BLANCHED PEANUTS, LIGHTLY
TOASTED

1. Lightly oil 42 silicone mini cupcake cases
and place on a large baking sheet. To make the
coating, sift together the cornflour and icing
sugar into a bowl. Use a little of this mixture to
dust each case.

2. Follow the basic recipe (see page 12) to make
the marshmallow. Fold in the nuts. Divide the
mixture between the prepared cases. Lightly
dust the tops with a little of the coating mixture.
Leave to set, uncovered, in a cool, dry place for
2-3 hours.

3. Carefully remove the marshmallows from the
cases. Lightly dust each one with the remaining
coating mixture.

4. To decorate, place the chocolate in a heatproof
bowl set over a saucepan of gently simmering
water and heat until melted. Remove from the
heat and stir until smooth. Leave to cool for
10 minutes.

5. Meanwhile, line a baking sheet with baking
paper. Holding each marshmallow by the base,
briefly dip the top in the melted chocolate, then
place on the prepared baking sheet. Top each
marshmallow with a few toasted peanuts and
leave in a cool place to set. Store in an airtight
container for up to 5 days.

1.

2.

5.

Mocha
MARSHMALLOWS

Makes: 24
Prep: 45 minutes (plus cooling)
Cook: 25 minutes
Set: 3-4 hours

Ingredients

SUNFLOWER OIL, FOR GREASING

1 TBSP CORNFLOUR

1 TBSP ICING SUGAR

200 ML/7 FL OZ COLD WATER

450 G/1 LB GRANULATED SUGAR

100 ML/3½ FL OZ HOT BLACK COFFEE, MADE WITH 2 TSP INSTANT ESPRESSO COFFEE GRANULES

25 G/1 OZ POWDERED GELATINE

2 LARGE EGG WHITES

1 TSP VANILLA EXTRACT

TO DECORATE

115 G/4 OZ PLAIN CHOCOLATE, BROKEN INTO PIECES

2 TBSP FINELY GRATED PLAIN CHOCOLATE

1. Lightly oil a 23 x 33-cm/9 x 13-inch Swiss roll tin. Line the base and two short sides with baking paper, then lightly oil the paper.

2. To make the coating, sift together the cornflour and icing sugar into a bowl. Use a little of this mixture to dust the lined tin, tapping it firmly so the mixture coats the base and sides completely.

3. Follow the basic recipe (see page 12) to make the marshmallow, dissolving the gelatine in the coffee.

4. Pour the mixture into the prepared tin and gently level the surface. Lightly dust the top with a little more of the coating mixture. Leave to set, uncovered, in a cool, dry place for 3-4 hours.

5. Run the tip of a lightly greased knife along the unlined sides of the tin to release the marshmallow. Using the lining paper, gently lift out the marshmallow sheet and place on a chopping board. Cut into 24 squares, wiping and re-greasing the knife frequently. Lightly dust the squares with the remaining coating mixture.

6. To decorate, break the chocolate into pieces and place in a heatproof bowl set over a saucepan of gently simmering water. Heat until melted. Remove from the heat and stir until smooth. Leave to cool for 10 minutes.

7. Half-dip each marshmallow square in the melted chocolate, shaking gently to allow the excess to run off. Sprinkle with the grated chocolate. Place on a baking sheet lined with baking paper and leave in a cool place to set. Store in an airtight container for up to 5 days.

3.

5.

7.

Chocolate & Hazelnut
MARSHMALLOWS

Makes: 25
Prep: 45 minutes (plus cooling)
Cook: 25 minutes
Set: 4–5 hours

Ingredients

SUNFLOWER OIL, FOR GREASING

1 TBSP CORNFLOUR

1 TBSP ICING SUGAR

200 ML/7 FL OZ COLD WATER

450 G/1 LB GRANULATED SUGAR

100 ML/3½ FL OZ HOT WATER

25 G/1 OZ POWDERED GELATINE

2 LARGE EGG WHITES

1 TSP VANILLA EXTRACT

3 TBSP CHOCOLATE AND HAZELNUT SPREAD, WARMED

25 BLANCHED HAZELNUTS, TOASTED

TO DECORATE

100 G/3½ OZ PLAIN CHOCOLATE, BROKEN INTO PIECES

1. Lightly oil a 20-cm/8-inch shallow square cake tin. Line the base and two sides with baking paper, then lightly oil the paper.

2. To make the coating, sift together the cornflour and icing sugar into a bowl. Use this mixture to dust the lined tin, tapping it firmly so the mixture coats the base and sides completely.

3. Follow the basic recipe (see page 12) to make the marshmallow. Gently fold in the warmed chocolate and hazelnut spread.

4. Pour the mixture into the prepared tin and gently level the surface. Lightly dust the top with some of the coating mixture, then arrange the hazelnuts evenly on top of the marshmallow. Leave to set, uncovered, in a cool, dry place for 4–5 hours.

5. Run the tip of a lightly greased knife along the unlined sides of the tin to release the marshmallow. Using the lining paper, gently lift out the marshmallow and place on a chopping board. Cut into 25 squares, wiping and re-greasing the knife frequently. Dust with the coating mixture.

6. To decorate, put the chocolate into a heatproof bowl set over a saucepan of gently simmering water and heat until melted. Remove from the heat and stir until smooth. Leave to cool for 10 minutes.

7. Spoon the chocolate into a paper piping bag and snip off the end. Pipe lines of chocolate over the marshmallows. Leave in a cool place to set. Store in an airtight container for up to 5 days.

3.

4.

7.

Cinnamon & Cocoa
MARSHMALLOWS

Makes: 36
Prep: 45 minutes
Cook: 20 minutes
Set: 4-5 hours

Ingredients

SUNFLOWER OIL, FOR GREASING

1 TBSP CORNFLOUR

1 TBSP ICING SUGAR

1/2 TSP COCOA POWDER

1/4 TSP GROUND CINNAMON

200 ML/7 FL OZ COLD WATER

450 G/1 LB GRANULATED SUGAR

100 ML/3 1/2 FL OZ HOT WATER

25 G/1 OZ POWDERED GELATINE

2 LARGE EGG WHITES

1 1/2 TSP GROUND CINNAMON

3 TBSP COCOA POWDER BLENDED TO A PASTE WITH 3 TBSP HOT WATER

1. Lightly oil a 20-cm/8-inch shallow square cake tin. Line the base and two sides with baking paper, then lightly oil the paper.

2. To make the coating, sift together the cornflour, icing sugar, cocoa powder and cinnamon into a bowl. Use a little of this mixture to dust the lined tin, tapping it firmly so the mixture coats the base and sides completely.

3. Follow the basic recipe (see page 12) to make the marshmallow, omitting the vanilla extract.

4. Transfer half the whisked marshmallow mixture to a separate bowl and gently fold in the ground cinnamon. Gradually fold the cocoa paste into the remaining mixture.

5. Drop alternate spoonfuls of the two mixtures into the prepared tin and gently level the surface. Swirl the two mixtures together with the tip of a knife. Leave to set, uncovered, in a cool, dry place for 4-5 hours.

6. Run the tip of a lightly greased knife along the unlined sides of the tin to release the marshmallow. Using the lining paper, gently lift out the marshmallow and place on a chopping board. Cut into 36 squares, wiping and re-greasing the knife frequently. Lightly dust the bars with the coating mixture. Store in an airtight container for up to 5 days.

2.

4.

5.

White Choc & Peppermint
MARSHMALLOWS

Makes: 24
Prep: 45 minutes
(plus cooling)
Cook: 25 minutes
Set: 3-4 hours

Ingredients

SUNFLOWER OIL, FOR GREASING

1 TBSP CORNFLOUR

1 TBSP ICING SUGAR

200 ML/7 FL OZ COLD WATER

450 G/1 LB GRANULATED SUGAR

100 ML/3½ FL OZ HOT WATER

25 G/1 OZ POWDERED GELATINE

2 LARGE EGG WHITES

FEW DROPS PEPPERMINT EXTRACT

100 G/3½ OZ WHITE CHOCOLATE,
BROKEN INTO PIECES

4 SMALL CANDY CANES, ROUGHLY
CRUSHED

1. Lightly oil two 12-hole silicone cupcake trays and place on 2 baking sheets. To make the coating, sift together the cornflour and icing sugar into a bowl. Use a little of this mixture to lightly dust each hole.

2. Follow the basic recipe (see page 12) to make the marshmallow, replacing the vanilla extract with the peppermint extract.

3. Put the chocolate into a heatproof bowl set over a saucepan of barely simmering water and heat until melted. Remove from the heat and stir until smooth. Leave to cool for 10 minutes, stirring occasionally.

4. Gently fold three quarters of the melted chocolate into the marshmallow mixture. Spoon the mixture into the prepared trays.

5. Spoon a small swirl of the remaining melted chocolate onto each marshmallow and sprinkle with the crushed candy canes. Lightly dust the tops with a little of the coating mixture. Leave to set, uncovered, in a cool, dry place for 3-4 hours.

6. Carefully remove the marshmallows from the trays. Lightly dust the base and sides with the remaining coating mixture. Store in an airtight container for up to 5 days.

3.

4.

5.

Toffee Bite
MARSHMALLOWS

Makes: 25
Prep: 45 minutes
Cook: 20 minutes
Set: 4-5 hours

Ingredients

SUNFLOWER OIL, FOR GREASING

1 TBSP CORNFLOUR

1 TBSP ICING SUGAR

200 ML/7 FL OZ COLD WATER

450 G/1 LB GRANULATED SUGAR

100 ML/3½ FL OZ HOT WATER

25 G/1 OZ POWDERED GELATINE

2 LARGE EGG WHITES

1 TSP VANILLA EXTRACT

8 TBSP DULCE DU LECHE

40 G/1½ OZ MILK CHOCOLATE CHIPS

1. Lightly oil a 20-cm/8-inch shallow square cake tin. Line the base and two sides with baking paper, then lightly oil the paper.

2. To make the coating, sift together the cornflour and icing sugar into a bowl. Use this mixture to dust the lined tin, tapping it firmly so the mixture coats the base and sides completely.

3. Follow the basic recipe (see page 12) to make the marshmallow. Gently fold in 3 tablespoons of the dulce du leche.

4. Pour one third of the marshmallow mixture into the prepared tin, then dot with tiny blobs of dulce du leche. Make two more layers with the remaining marshmallow and dulce du leche, then drag a skewer through the marshmallow to create a swirled effect.

5. Scatter over the chocolate chips. Lightly dust the top with a little of the coating mixture. Leave to set, uncovered, in a cool, dry place for 4-5 hours.

6. Run the tip of a lightly greased knife along the unlined sides of the tin to release the marshmallow. Using the lining paper, gently lift out the marshmallow and place on a chopping board.

7. Cut into 25 squares, wiping and re-greasing the knife frequently. Lightly dust the squares with the remaining coating mixture. Store in an airtight container for up to 5 days.

4.

5.

7.

Cookie Sandwich
MARSHMALLOWS

Makes: 20
Prep: 1 hour 15 mins
(plus chilling & cooling)
Cook: 40 minutes
Set: 3-4 hours

Ingredients

SUNFLOWER OIL, FOR GREASING

1 TBSP CORNFLOUR

1 TBSP ICING SUGAR

200 ML/7 FL OZ COLD WATER

450 G/1 LB GRANULATED SUGAR

100 ML/3½ FL OZ HOT WATER

25 G/1 OZ POWDERED GELATINE

2 LARGE EGG WHITES

1 TSP VANILLA EXTRACT

COOKIES

115 G/4 OZ BUTTER, SOFTENED, PLUS EXTRA FOR GREASING

55 G/2 OZ CASTER SUGAR

1 EGG YOLK

175 G/6 OZ PLAIN FLOUR, PLUS EXTRA FOR DUSTING

250 G/9 OZ PLAIN CHOCOLATE, BROKEN INTO PIECES

1. Lightly oil a 23 x 33-cm/9 x 13-inch Swiss roll tin. Line the base and two short sides with baking paper then lightly oil the paper.

2. To make the coating, sift together the cornflour and icing sugar into a bowl. Use a little of this mixture to dust the lined tin, tapping it firmly so the mixture coats the base and sides completely.

3. Follow the basic recipe (see page 12) to make the marshmallow. Pour the mixture into the prepared tin and gently level the surface. Lightly dust the top with a little of the coating mixture. Leave to set, uncovered, in a cool, dry place for 3-4 hours.

4. Meanwhile, make the cookies. Put the butter and sugar into a bowl and beat with an electric mixer until pale and creamy. Beat in the egg yolk, then sift in the flour and mix to a soft dough. Knead lightly until smooth, then wrap in clingfilm and chill in the refrigerator for 45 minutes.

5. Preheat the oven to 180°C/350°F/Gas Mark 4. Grease two large baking sheets. Roll the dough out on a lightly floured work surface to about 5 mm/¼ inch thick and use a 6-cm/2½-inch cloud-shaped cutter to stamp out 40 cookies, re-rolling the dough as necessary. Place on the prepared baking sheets and chill in the refrigerator for 30 minutes.

...CONTINUES ON PAGE 44

6.

7.

9.

6. Bake in the preheated oven for 10-12 minutes or until pale golden. Leave to cool on the sheets for 1-2 minutes, then transfer to a wire rack to cool completely.

7. Put the chocolate into a heatproof bowl set over a saucepan of gently simmering water and heat until melted. Remove from the heat and stir until smooth. Leave to cool for 10 minutes. Dip one side of each cookie in the melted chocolate, then place on a wire rack set over a baking sheet. Chill in the refrigerator until set.

8. To assemble the sandwich cookies, run the tip of a lightly greased knife along the unlined sides of the tin to release the marshmallow. Using the lining paper, gently lift out the marshmallow sheet and slide onto a chopping board.

9. Lightly grease the cloud cutter and use to stamp out 20 cloud shapes, washing, drying and re-greasing the cutter frequently. Toss all the cloud shapes in the remaining coating mixture. Sandwich each marshmallow between two of the chocolate-coated cookies. Store in an airtight container for up to 5 days.

OUR CRISP, CHOCOLATEY COOKIES ARE CLOUD-SHAPED, BUT YOU CAN USE ANY SIMPLE COOKIE CUTTER FOR BOTH THE BISCUIT BASE AND THE MARSHMALLOW MIDDLE.

Pina Colada
MARSHMALLOWS

Makes: 35
Prep: 45 minutes
Cook: 20 minutes
Set: 4-5 hours

Ingredients

SUNFLOWER OIL, FOR GREASING

1 TSP CORNFLOUR

1 TSP ICING SUGAR

100 G/3½ OZ DESICCATED COCONUT

PINK FOOD COLOURING PASTE

100 ML/3½ FL OZ PINEAPPLE JUICE

100 ML/3½ FL OZ COLD WATER

450 G/1 LB GRANULATED SUGAR

100 ML/3½ FL OZ HOT WATER

25 G/1 OZ POWDERED GELATINE

2 LARGE EGG WHITES

2 TBSP COCONUT LIQUEUR OR RUM, WARMED

YELLOW FOOD COLOURING PASTE

1. Lightly oil a 18 x 28-cm/7 x 11-inch traybake tin. Line the base and two short sides with baking paper, then lightly oil the paper.

2. To make the coating, sift together the cornflour and icing sugar into a bowl. Use a little of this mixture to dust the lined tin, tapping it firmly so the mixture coats the base and sides completely.

3. Place the coconut in a resealable polythene bag with a tiny amount of pink food colouring paste. Seal the bag and rub it thoroughly between the palms of your hands until the coconut is evenly coloured pale pink. Sprinkle half the coconut in the base of the tin, reserving the remainder.

4. Follow the basic recipe (see page 12) to make the marshmallow, replacing half the cold water for the sugar syrup with the pineapple juice and omitting the vanilla extract. Whisk in the liqueur and then whisk in a little food colouring paste to turn the mixture pale yellow.

5. Pour the mixture into the prepared tin. Level the surface and sprinkle over the remaining pink coconut to cover the top completely, pressing down gently. Leave to set, uncovered, in a cool, dry place for 4–5 hours.

6. Run the tip of a lightly greased knife along the unlined sides of the tin to release the marshmallow. Using the lining paper, gently lift out the marshmallow and place on a chopping board. Cut into 35 squares, wiping and re-greasing the knife frequently. Store in an airtight container for up to 5 days.

3.

4.

6.

Mojito
MARSHMALLOWS

Makes: 25
Prep: 45 minutes
(plus cooling)
Cook: 30 minutes
Set: 4-5 hours

Ingredients

SUNFLOWER OIL, FOR GREASING

1 TBSP CORNFLOUR

1 TBSP ICING SUGAR

200 ML/7 FL OZ COLD WATER

5 FRESH MINT STEMS

JUICE OF 1 LARGE LIME

450 G/1 LB GRANULATED SUGAR

25 G/1 OZ POWDERED GELATINE

2 LARGE EGG WHITES

1 TBSP WHITE RUM, WARMED

GREEN FOOD COLOURING PASTE

1 TSP FINELY GRATED LIME ZEST

1 TSP FINELY CHOPPED FRESH MINT

1. Lightly oil a 20-cm/8-inch shallow square cake tin. Line the base and two sides with baking paper, then lightly oil the paper.

2. To make the coating, sift together the cornflour and icing sugar into a bowl. Use this mixture to dust the lined tin, tapping it firmly so the mixture coats the base and sides completely.

3. Put the water and mint into a saucepan over a low heat and heat until almost boiling. Remove from the heat and leave to cool completely. Strain into a measuring jug, topping up with cold water to make 200 ml/7 fl oz. Pour the lime juice into a measuring jug and add enough boiling water to make 100 ml/3½ fl oz liquid. Pour into a small saucepan and heat over a low heat.

4. Follow the basic recipe (see page 12) to make the marshmallow, using the mint-infused water for the syrup. Dissolve the gelatine in the hot lime juice mixture and omit the vanilla extract. Whisk in the rum and a little food colouring paste to colour the marshmallow pale green. Fold in the lime zest and chopped mint.

5. Pour the mixture into the prepared tin and gently level the surface. Lightly dust the top with a little of the coating mixture. Leave to set, uncovered, in a cool, dry place for 4-5 hours.

6. Run the tip of a lightly greased knife along the unlined sides of the tin to release the marshmallow. Using the lining paper, gently lift out the marshmallow and place on a chopping board. Cut into 25 squares, wiping and re-greasing the knife frequently. Lightly dust the squares with the coating mixture. Store in an airtight container for up to 5 days.

48

3.

4.

5.

49

Bourbon & Brown Sugar
MARSHMALLOWS

Makes: 24
Prep: 40 minutes
Cook: 20 minutes
Set: 3-4 hours

Ingredients

SUNFLOWER OIL, FOR GREASING

1 TBSP CORNFLOUR

1 TBSP ICING SUGAR

200 ML/7 FL OZ COLD WATER

450 G/1 LB GRANULATED SUGAR

100 ML/3½ FL OZ HOT WATER

25 G/1 OZ POWDERED GELATINE

2 LARGE EGG WHITES

1 TSP VANILLA EXTRACT

2 TBSP BOURBON, WARMED

4 TBSP DEMERARA SUGAR

1. Lightly oil a 23 x 33-cm/9 x 13-inch Swiss roll tin. Line the base and two short sides with baking paper, then lightly oil the paper.

2. To make the coating, sift together the cornflour and icing sugar into a bowl. Use a little of this mixture to dust the lined tin, tapping it firmly so the mixture coats the base and sides completely.

3. Follow the basic recipe (see page 12) to make the marshmallow. Gradually whisk in the bourbon.

4. Pour the mixture into the prepared tin and gently level the surface. Lightly dust the top with a little of the coating mixture. Leave to set, uncovered, in a cool, dry place for 3-4 hours.

5. Run the tip of a lightly greased knife along the sides of the tin to release the marshmallow. Using the lining paper, gently lift out the marshmallow sheet and place on a chopping board.

6. Lightly grease a 5-cm/2-inch round cutter and stamp out 24 rounds, washing, drying and re-greasing the cutter frequently. Lightly dust the top and bottom of the marshmallows with the remaining coating mixture.

7. Place the demerara sugar on a flat plate. Roll the edge of each marshmallow round in the sugar to coat. Store in an airtight container for up to 5 days.

6.

7.

3.

Amaretto Crunch
MARSHMALLOWS

Ingredients

SUNFLOWER OIL, FOR GREASING

1 TSP CORNFLOUR

1 TSP ICING SUGAR

85 G/3 OZ AMARETTI BISCUITS, CRUSHED

200 ML/7 FL OZ COLD WATER

450 G/1 LB GRANULATED SUGAR

100 ML/3½ FL OZ HOT WATER

25 G/1 OZ POWDERED GELATINE

2 LARGE EGG WHITES

1 TBSP AMARETTO LIQUEUR, WARMED

1. Lightly oil a 20-cm/8-inch shallow square cake tin. Line the base and two sides with baking paper, then lightly oil the paper.

2. To make the coating, sift together the cornflour and icing sugar into a bowl. Use this mixture to dust the lined tin, tapping it firmly so the mixture coats the base and sides completely. Spread one third of the crushed biscuits in an even layer in the base of the tin.

3. Follow the basic recipe (see page 12) to make the marshmallow, omitting the vanilla extract. Gradually whisk in the liqueur.

4. Pour the mixture into the prepared tin and gently level the surface. Scatter a further one third of the crushed biscuits over the top to cover the surface. Leave to set, uncovered, in a cool, dry place for 4-5 hours.

5. Run the tip of a lightly greased knife along the unlined sides of the tin to release the marshmallow. Using the lining paper, gently lift out the marshmallow and place on a chopping board.

6. Cut the marshmallow into 25 squares, wiping and re-greasing the knife frequently. Coat the squares in the remaining crushed biscuits. Store in an airtight container for up to 5 days.

Irish Cream
MARSHMALLOWS

Makes: 20
Prep: 45 minutes
(plus cooling)
Cook: 25 minutes
Set: 3-4 hours

Ingredients

SUNFLOWER OIL, FOR GREASING

1 TBSP CORNFLOUR

1 TBSP ICING SUGAR

200 ML/7 FL OZ COLD WATER

450 G/1 LB GRANULATED SUGAR

100 ML/3½ FL OZ HOT WATER

25 G/1 OZ POWDERED GELATINE

2 LARGE EGG WHITES

2 TBSP IRISH CREAM LIQUEUR, WARMED

TO DECORATE

200 G/7 OZ PLAIN CHOCOLATE,
BROKEN INTO PIECES

COCOA POWDER, FOR DUSTING

1. Lightly oil a 23 x 33-cm/9 x 13-inch Swiss roll tin. Line the base and two short sides with baking paper, then lightly oil the paper.

2. To make the coating, sift together the cornflour and icing sugar into a bowl. Use a little of this mixture to dust the lined tin, tapping it firmly so the mixture coats the base and sides completely.

3. Follow the basic recipe (see page 12) to make the marshmallow, omitting the vanilla extract. Gradually whisk in the liqueur.

4. Pour the mixture into the prepared tin and gently level the surface. Lightly dust the top with a little of the coating mixture. Leave to set, uncovered, in a cool, dry place for 3-4 hours.

5. Run the tip of a lightly greased knife along the unlined sides of the tin to release the marshmallow. Using the lining paper gently lift out the marshmallow sheet and place on a chopping board.

6. Lightly grease a 6-cm/2½-inch heart-shaped cutter. Use to stamp out 20 heart shapes, washing, drying and re-greasing the cutter frequently. Toss the hearts in the coating mixture.

7. To decorate, put the chocolate into a heatproof bowl set over a saucepan of gently simmering water and heat until melted. Remove from the heat and stir until smooth. Leave to cool for 10 minutes.

8. Dip one side of each marshmallow in the melted chocolate to coat. Place on a baking sheet lined with baking paper and leave in a cool place to set. Dust lightly with a little cocoa powder. Store in an airtight container for up to 5 days.

4.

6.

8.

Egg Nog
MARSHMALLOWS

Makes: 24
Prep: 40 minutes
Cook: 20 minutes
Set: 3-4 hours

Ingredients

SUNFLOWER OIL, FOR GREASING

1 TBSP CORNFLOUR

1 TBSP ICING SUGAR

200 ML/7 FL OZ COLD WATER

450 G/1 LB GRANULATED SUGAR

100 ML/3½ FL OZ HOT WATER

25 G/1 OZ POWDERED GELATINE

2 LARGE EGG WHITES

1 TSP VANILLA EXTRACT

1½ TBSP BRANDY, WARMED

1 TSP GROUND CINNAMON

1 TSP GRATED NUTMEG

1. Lightly oil 24 star-shaped silicone cupcake cases and place on a large baking sheet. To make the coating, sift together the cornflour and icing sugar into a bowl. Use a little of this mixture to dust each case.

2. Follow the basic recipe (see page 12) to make the marshmallow. Gradually whisk in the brandy and half the cinnamon and nutmeg. Spoon the mixture into the prepared cases.

3. Mix together the remaining cinnamon and nutmeg and sprinkle a little on top of each marshmallow. Using a cocktail stick, gently swirl the spices through the marshmallow. Lightly dust the tops with a little of the coating mixture. Leave to set, uncovered, in a cool, dry place for 3-4 hours.

4. Carefully remove the marshmallows from the cases. Lightly dust the base and sides of each one with the remaining coating mixture. Store in an airtight container for up to 5 days.

FLOAT A COUPLE OF THESE MINI MARSHMALLOWS ON TOP OF A MUG OF HOT CHOCOLATE, WITH PLENTY OF WHIPPED CREAM — IT'S DELISH!

Rum & Raisin
MARSHMALLOWS

Makes: 35
Prep: 40 minutes
(plus soaking)
Cook: 20 minutes
Set: 4-5 hours

Ingredients

85 G/3 OZ RAISINS

2 TBSP DARK RUM, WARMED

SUNFLOWER OIL, FOR GREASING

1 TBSP CORNFLOUR

1 TBSP ICING SUGAR

200 ML/7 FL OZ COLD WATER

450 G/1 LB GRANULATED SUGAR

100 ML/3½ FL OZ HOT WATER

25 G/1 OZ POWDERED GELATINE

2 LARGE EGG WHITES

2 TSP COFFEE AND CHICORY ESSENCE

1. Place the raisins and rum in a small bowl and leave to soak for 2 hours.

2. Lightly oil a 18 x 28-cm/7 x 11-inch traybake tin. Line the base and two short sides with baking paper, then lightly oil the paper.

3. To make the coating, sift together the cornflour and icing sugar into a bowl. Use a little of this mixture to dust the lined tin, tapping it firmly so the mixture coats the base and sides completely.

4. Follow the basic recipe (see page 12) to make the marshmallow, replacing the vanilla extract with the coffee and chicory essence.

5. Drain the raisins and fold half of them into the marshmallow, then pour the mixture into the prepared tin. Level the surface and scatter over the remaining raisins. Lightly dust the top with some of the coating mixture. Leave to set, uncovered, in a cool, dry place for 4-5 hours.

6. Run the tip of a lightly greased knife along the unlined sides of the tin to release the marshmallow. Using the lining paper, gently lift out the marshmallow and place on a chopping board. Cut into 35 squares, wiping and re-greasing the knife frequently. Lightly dust the squares with the remaining coating mixture. Store in an airtight container for up to 5 days.

1.

4.

5.

Toffee Apple
MARSHMALLOW POPS

Makes: 36
Prep: 50 minutes
(plus cooling)
Cook: 25 minutes
Set: 4-5 hours

Ingredients

SUNFLOWER OIL, FOR GREASING

1 TBSP CORNFLOUR

1 TBSP ICING SUGAR

100 ML/3½ FL OZ COLD WATER

100 ML/3½ FL OZ APPLE JUICE

450 G/1 LB GRANULATED SUGAR

100 ML/3½ FL OZ HOT WATER

25 G/1 OZ POWDERED GELATINE

2 LARGE EGG WHITES

1½ TSP GROUND CINNAMON

CARAMEL

115 G/4 OZ GRANULATED SUGAR

3 TBSP COLD WATER

YOU WILL ALSO NEED

36 LOLLIPOP STICKS (OPTIONAL)

1. Lightly oil or spray a 20-cm/8-inch shallow cake tin. Line the base and sides with baking paper then lightly oil the paper.

2. To make the coating, sift together the cornflour and icing sugar into a bowl. Use a little of this mixture to dust the lined tin, tapping it firmly so the mixture coats the base and sides completely.

3. Follow the basic recipe (see page 12) to make the marshmallow replacing half the cold water for the sugar syrup with apple juice and omitting the vanilla extract.

4. Pour the mixture into the prepared tin and gently level the surface. Sprinkle over the cinnamon then lightly dust the top with a little of the coating mixture. Leave to set, uncovered, in a cool, dry place for 4-5 hours.

5. Using the lining paper gently lift out the marshmallow and place on a chopping board. Cut into 36 squares with a lightly greased knife, wiping and re-greasing the knife frequently. Dust the squares lightly with the remaining coating mixture. Place the marshmallows on a baking sheet lined with baking paper.

...CONTINUES ON PAGE 62

ADD SOME CRUNCH BY SPRINKLING CRUSHED BISCUITS ON TOP OF THE CARAMEL – GINGER NUTS GIVE A DELICIOUS CRISP BITE.

5.

6.

7.

6. To make the caramel, place the sugar and water in a small heavy-based saucepan and heat gently, stirring, until the sugar has dissolved. Increase the heat and boil rapidly for 3-4 minutes, without stirring, until the syrup turns to a golden caramel. Swirl the pan to ensure even cooking. Remove from the heat and leave for 1-2 minutes.

7. Using a spoon, quickly drizzle the hot caramel over the marshmallows (take care because the caramel will be extremely hot). Leave in a cool place until the caramel has set. Lift each marshmallow from the baking sheet and gently push a lollipop stick into each one, if using. Serve within a few hours of decorating.

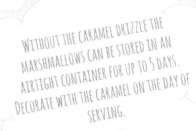

WITHOUT THE CARAMEL DRIZZLE THE MARSHMALLOWS CAN BE STORED IN AN AIRTIGHT CONTAINER FOR UP TO 5 DAYS. DECORATE WITH THE CARAMEL ON THE DAY OF SERVING.

Pumpkin & Pecan
MARSHMALLOWS

Ingredients

SUNFLOWER OIL, FOR GREASING

2 TSP CORNFLOUR

2 TSP ICING SUGAR

200 ML/7 FL OZ COLD WATER

450 G/1 LB GRANULATED SUGAR

100 ML/3½ FL OZ HOT WATER

25 G/1 OZ POWDERED GELATINE

2 LARGE EGG WHITES

1 TSP VANILLA EXTRACT

115 G/4 OZ PUMPKIN PURÉE, WARMED

2 TSP GROUND MIXED SPICE

ORANGE FOOD COLOURING PASTE

SUGAR-COATED PECANS

1 TBSP EGG WHITE, BEATEN

1 TSP VANILLA EXTRACT

55 G/2 OZ LIGHT MUSCOVADO SUGAR

85 G/3 OZ PECAN NUTS

1. Lightly oil a 20-cm/8-inch shallow square cake tin. Line the base and two sides with baking paper, then lightly oil the paper.

2. To make the coating, sift together the cornflour and icing sugar into a bowl. Use this mixture to dust the lined tin, tapping it firmly so the mixture coats the base and sides completely.

3. Follow the basic recipe (see page 12) to make the marshmallow. Gently fold in the warmed pumpkin puree and mixed spice. Fold in a little food colouring paste to colour the mixture deep orange.

4. Pour the mixture into the prepared tin and gently level the surface. Lightly dust the top with some of the coating mixture. Leave to set, uncovered, in a cool, dry place for 4-5 hours.

5. Meanwhile, make the sugar-coated pecan nuts. Preheat the oven to 150°C/300°F/Gas Mark 2. Line a baking sheet with baking paper. Mix together the egg white, vanilla extract and sugar in a small bowl, then add the nuts and stir to coat. Spread the coated nuts evenly on the prepared tray. Bake in the preheated oven for 25-30 minutes, turning once, until crisp and golden. Leave to cool completely.

6. Run the tip of a lightly greased knife along the unlined sides of the tin to release the marshmallow. Using the lining paper, gently lift out the marshmallow and place on a chopping board. Cut into 25 squares, wiping and re-greasing the knife frequently.

7. Finely chop the sugar-coated nuts and spread on a flat plate. Dip every side of each marshmallow in the chopped nuts to coat. Serve on the day of decorating.

3.

5.

7.

Undecorated, the marshmallows
will keep in an airtight container for up
to 5 days. The sugar-coated pecans will keep in an
airtight container for up to 1 week.

Peanut Butter & Jelly
MARSHMALLOWS

Makes: 25
Prep: 40 minutes
Cook: 20 minutes
Set: 4-5 hours

Ingredients

SUNFLOWER OIL, FOR GREASING

1 TBSP CORNFLOUR

1 TBSP ICING SUGAR

200 ML/7 FL OZ COLD WATER

450 G/1 LB GRANULATED SUGAR

100 ML/3½ FL OZ HOT WATER

25 G/1 OZ POWDERED GELATINE

2 LARGE EGG WHITES

1 TSP VANILLA EXTRACT

4 TBSP CRUNCHY PEANUT BUTTER, SOFTENED

3 TBSP SEEDLESS RASPBERRY JAM

25 G/1 OZ BLANCHED PEANUTS, TOASTED AND CHOPPED

1. Lightly oil a 20-cm/8-inch shallow square cake tin. Line the base and two sides with baking paper, then lightly oil the paper.

2. To make the coating, sift together the cornflour and icing sugar into a bowl. Use a little of this mixture to dust the lined tin, tapping it firmly so the mixture coats the base and sides completely.

3. Follow the basic recipe (see page 12) to make the marshmallow. Gently fold in the peanut butter.

4. Pour half the mixture into the prepared tin, then top with 1 tablespoon of the jam and swirl through the mixture with the tip of a knife. Repeat with the remaining marshmallow mixture and the remaining jam.

5. Swirl the jam through the marshmallow with the tip of a knife. Scatter over the chopped peanuts. Lightly dust the top with a little of the coating mixture. Leave to set, uncovered, in a cool, dry place for 4-5 hours.

6. Run the tip of a lightly greased knife along the unlined sides of the tin to release the marshmallow. Using the lining paper, gently lift out the marshmallow and place on a chopping board. Cut into 25 squares, wiping and re-greasing the knife frequently. Lightly dust the squares with the remaining coating mixture. Store in an airtight container for up to 5 days.

4.

5.

Gingerbread
MARSHMALLOWS

Makes: 24
Prep: 40 minutes
Cook: 20 minutes
Set: 3-4 hours

Ingredients

SUNFLOWER OIL, FOR GREASING

1 TBSP CORNFLOUR

1 TBSP ICING SUGAR

2 TSP GROUND GINGER

200 ML/7 FL OZ COLD WATER

225 G/8 OZ GRANULATED SUGAR

225 G/8 OZ LIGHT MUSCOVADO SUGAR

100 ML/3½ FL OZ HOT WATER

25 G/1 OZ POWDERED GELATINE

2 LARGE EGG WHITES

1. Lightly oil a 23 x 33-cm/9 x 13-inch Swiss roll tin. Line the base and two short sides with baking paper, then lightly oil the paper.

2. To make the coating, sift together the cornflour, icing sugar and 1 teaspoon of ground ginger into a bowl. Use a little of this mixture to dust the lined tin, tapping it firmly so the mixture coats the base and sides completely.

3. Follow the basic recipe (see page 12) to make the marshmallow, replacing half the granulated sugar with muscovado sugar and omitting the vanilla extract. Fold in the remaining ground ginger.

4. Pour the mixture into the prepared tin and gently level the surface. Lightly dust the top with a little of the coating mixture. Leave to set, uncovered, in a cool, dry place for 3-4 hours.

5. Run the tip of a lightly greased knife along the unlined sides of the tin to release the marshmallow. Using the lining paper, gently lift out the marshmallow sheet and place on a chopping board.

6. Lightly grease a small gingerbread man cookie cutter. Use to stamp out 24 shapes, washing, drying and re-greasing the cutter frequently. Toss the gingerbread men in the coating mixture. Store in an airtight container for up to 5 days.

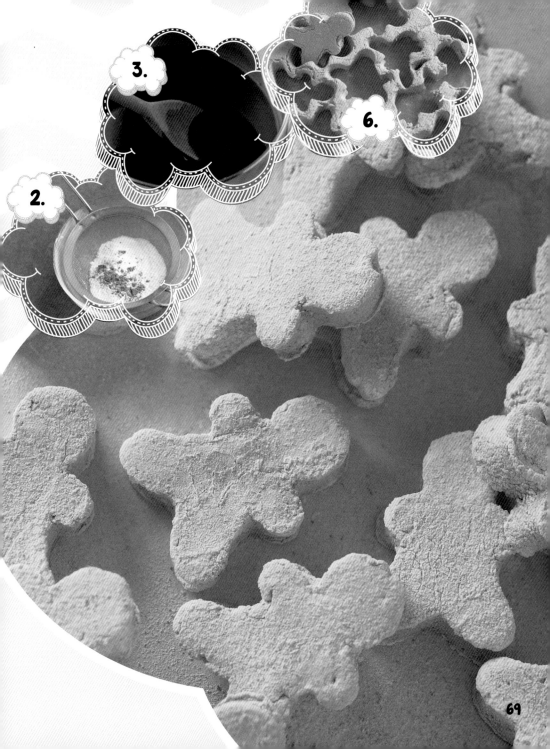

3.

2.

6.

Cookies & Cream
MARSHMALLOWS

Makes: 35
Prep: 40 minutes
Cook: 20 minutes
Set: 4–5 hours

Ingredients

SUNFLOWER OIL, FOR GREASING

1 TSP CORNFLOUR

1 TSP ICING SUGAR

18 SMALL DOUBLE CHOCOLATE CHIP COOKIES

200 ML/7 FL OZ COLD WATER

450 G/1 LB GRANULATED SUGAR

100 ML/3½ FL OZ HOT WATER

25 G/1 OZ POWDERED GELATINE

2 LARGE EGG WHITES

1 TSP VANILLA EXTRACT

1. Lightly oil a 18 x 28-cm/7 x 11-inch traybake tin. Line the base and two short sides with baking paper, then lightly oil the paper.

2. To make the coating, sift together the cornflour and icing sugar into a bowl. Use a little of this mixture to dust the lined tin, tapping it firmly so the mixture coats the base and sides completely.

3. Arrange 15 of the cookies in the base of the prepared tin. Finely crush the remaining cookies and set aside.

4. Follow the basic recipe (see page 12) to make the marshmallow. Pour the mixture into the tin. Level the surface and sprinkle over the crushed cookies to cover the top completely. Leave to set, uncovered, in a cool, dry place for 4–5 hours.

5. Run the tip of a lightly greased knife along the unlined sides of the tin to release the marshmallow. Using the lining paper, gently lift out the marshmallow and place on a chopping board. Cut into 35 squares, wiping and re-greasing the knife frequently. Store in an airtight container for up to 5 days.

3.

4.

5.

S'mores
MARSHMALLOW POPS

Makes: 25
Prep: 50 minutes
(plus cooling)
Cook: 30 minutes
Set: 4-5 hours

Ingredients

SUNFLOWER OIL, FOR GREASING

1 TBSP CORNFLOUR

1 TBSP ICING SUGAR

200 ML/7 FL OZ COLD WATER

450 G/1 LB GRANULATED SUGAR

100 ML/3½ FL OZ HOT WATER

25 G/1 OZ POWDERED GELATINE

2 LARGE EGG WHITES

1 TSP VANILLA EXTRACT

TO DECORATE

150 G/5½ OZ MILK CHOCOLATE,
BROKEN INTO PIECES

2 DIGESTIVE BISCUITS, FINELY CRUSHED

YOU WILL ALSO NEED

25 LOLLIPOP STICKS

1. Lightly oil an 18-cm/7-inch square cake tin (at least 5 cm/2 inches deep). Line the base and sides with baking paper, then lightly oil the paper.

2. To make the coating, sift together the cornflour and icing sugar into a bowl. Use a little of this mixture to dust the lined tin, tapping it firmly so the mixture coats the base and sides completely.

3. Follow the basic recipe (see page 12) to make the marshmallow. Pour the mixture into the prepared tin and gently level the surface. Lightly dust the top with a little of the coating mixture. Leave to set, uncovered, in a cool, dry place for 4-5 hours.

4. Run the tip of a lightly greased knife along the unlined sides of the tin to release the marshmallow. Using the lining paper, gently lift out the marshmallow and place on a chopping board. Cut into 25 squares with a lightly greased knife, wiping and re-greasing the knife frequently. Lightly dust the squares with the remaining coating mixture.

5. Lightly toast the marshmallows under a medium-hot grill, turning frequently until just golden (do this very briefly or they will melt and lose their shape). Alternatively, use a cook's blowtorch. Leave to cool.

...CONTINUES ON PAGE 74

5.

6.

7.

6. To decorate, place the chocolate in a heatproof bowl set over a saucepan of gently simmering water and heat until melted. Remove from the heat and stir until smooth. Leave to cool for 10 minutes.

7. Meanwhile, line a board with baking paper. Dip one end of each marshmallow in the melted chocolate, turning to coat, then shaking gently to allow the excess to run off. Sprinkle the chocolate with crushed biscuits, then place on the prepared board. Leave in a cool place to set. Gently push a lollipop stick into the chocolate end of each marshmallow. Store in an airtight container for up to 5 days.

A CLASSIC CAMPFIRE COMBO – CHOCOLATE, MARSHMALLOW AND DIGESTIVE BISCUIT IS HARD TO BEAT!

CLASSIC COMBO

Zesty Lemon
MARSHMALLOWS

Makes: 36
Prep: 45 minutes
Cook: 20 minutes
Set: 4-5 hours

Ingredients

SUNFLOWER OIL, FOR GREASING

1 TBSP CORNFLOUR

1 TBSP ICING SUGAR

200 ML/7 FL OZ COLD WATER

450 G/1 LB GRANULATED SUGAR

25 G/1 OZ POWDERED GELATINE

100 ML/3½ FL OZ HOT LEMON JUICE

2 LARGE EGG WHITES

FINELY GRATED ZEST OF 1 LEMON

YELLOW FOOD COLOURING PASTE

2 TBSP WHITE HUNDREDS AND THOUSANDS

1. Lightly oil a 20-cm/8-inch shallow square cake tin. Line the base and two sides with baking paper, then lightly oil the paper.

2. To make the coating, sift together the cornflour and icing sugar into a bowl. Use this mixture to dust the lined tin, tapping it firmly so the mixture coats the base and sides completely.

3. Follow the basic recipe (see page 12) to make the marshmallow, dissolving the gelatine in the hot lemon juice instead of hot water and omitting the vanilla extract.

4. Transfer one third of the whisked mixture to a separate bowl and set aside. Fold the lemon zest into the remaining mixture and whisk in a little food colouring paste to colour it pale yellow.

5. Pour the yellow mixture into the prepared tin and level the surface, then spoon the white mixture over the top and gently level with a small palette knife. Sprinkle over the hundreds and thousands, then lightly dust the top with a little of the coating mixture. Leave to set, uncovered, in a cool, dry place for 4-5 hours.

6. Run the tip of a lightly greased knife along the unlined sides of the tin to release the marshmallow. Using the lining paper, gently lift out the marshmallow and place on a chopping board. Cut into 36 squares, wiping and re-greasing the knife frequently. Lightly dust the squares with the remaining coating mixture. Store in an airtight container for up to 5 days.

3.

5.

6.

HOME-MADE
pillows OF
SUGAR

This edition published by Parragon Books Ltd in 2013
LOVE FOOD is an imprint of Parragon Books Ltd

Parragon Books Ltd
Chartist House
15–17 Trim Street
Bath BA1 1HA, UK
www.parragon.com/lovefood

ISBN 978-1-4723-2917-2

Printed in China

Project managed by Alice Blackledge
Designed by Beth Kalynka
Recipes, introduction and food styling by Angela Drake
Photography by Clive Streeter
Edited by Fiona Biggs

Notes for the Reader
This book uses both metric and imperial measurements. Follow the same units of measurement throughout; do not mix metric and imperial. All spoon measurements are level: teaspoons are assumed to be 5 ml, and tablespoons are assumed to be 15 ml. Unless otherwise stated, milk is assumed to be full fat and eggs are medium.

The times given are an approximate guide only. Preparation times differ according to the techniques used by different people and the cooking times may also vary from those given.

Recipes using raw or very lightly cooked eggs should be avoided by infants, the elderly, pregnant women, convalescents and anyone suffering from an illness. Pregnant and breastfeeding women are advised to avoid eating peanuts and peanut products. Sufferers from nut allergies should be aware that some of the ready-made ingredients used in the recipes in this book may contain nuts. Always check the packaging before use.

Front cover recipe: Basic Vanilla Marshmallows (page 12).